WHAT
NEED TO KNOW
ABOUT ALCOHOL

How to Help Yourself and Understand Others

FIONA STEELE

DEDICATION

This book is dedicated to
my mother for always believing in my abilities to
write a book, my father for his unquestioning
support throughout my life, and my partner,
Johnny, for encouraging me to follow my dreams
(and for looking after the dogs while I write).

CONTENTS

ACKNOWLEDGEMENTS

Thanks to my best friend,
Claire McMullan,
for her enthusiastic feedback, help with editing, and for
knowing me like no one else and still being my friend.

Thanks also go to
Kathleen Finnerty and Jordanna Kalla
for their feedback, encouragement and support.

Acknowledgements to
Dr Rachel Herring and Dr Karen Duke of
The Drug and Alcohol Research Centre at
Middlesex University, London
for their inspiration and support in helping me to
obtain my Master's degree in
Comparative Drug and Alcohol Studies.

PREFACE

Alcohol and other drugs have been a part of my life, both personally and professionally for over twenty years. My own experiences of using alcohol and drugs heavily in my younger years became my foundation for choosing a career supporting others with substance use problems, eventually providing training for other professionals working in the field and being awarded my Master of Arts degree in Drug and Alcohol Studies.

By combining my personal, professional, training and academic knowledge on the subject, I have gained valuable insight into how people can understand and manage their substance use in more satisfying ways than they do now. I have worked alongside many different women and men of all ages from varying social backgrounds and using a wide variety of drugs. I understand that local services offered to people with alcohol and drug problems can be less than satisfactory or the cost involved can keep specialist support out of reach. I also know that even with the best services available at no cost, there will be many people out there who will never go to an alcohol support service for one reason or another.

The good news is that for the majority of people who feel they need to take better control of their drinking this is entirely possible if they are to practice the advice and guidance contained within these pages sincerely. I have compiled this book to offer a quick and accessible guide on everything you need to know about alcohol with an overview of the impact drinking can have on our lives and why people use alcohol in the way that they do. The book contains a range of useful strategies you can put into action immediately and over the longer term to improve your general satisfaction with life.

If you are reading this book to help you understand somebody else's drinking, you will also gain valuable insight and learn better ways in which you might relate to this person. While each chapter is packed full of the information you need to know about alcohol, there are many subjects I have not covered in great depth in an effort to remain concise. You can find more resources and links to further information on the topics covered within the book on my website www.fionasteele.com where you can learn more about the subjects which interest you.

This book will give you the tools to go a long way in managing your alcohol use by yourself, in a similar way to how you may receive support from a professional. The guidance and strategies contained within each chapter may be new to you, or they may already be familiar but either way, they will not change anything for you unless you decide to implement them in your life. Whether you use the tools in this book, attend an alcohol support group, or you speak with a professional-

YOU are the only person that can make the necessary changes in your life to gain control over your alcohol use.

CHAPTER ONE:
WOMEN AND ALCOHOL

The rise of women drinking.

Heavy use of alcohol has been a feature of many European societies since medieval times and probably long before. Men and women of all ages drank alcohol daily as the fermentation process was a vital way in which to purify dirty water. Heavy alcohol use became more problematic for societies during the Industrial Revolution when many women joined the Temperance Movement, calling for a ban on alcohol sales altogether. While not always the case, until the last 30 years, heavy alcohol use has been associated more often with men and, statistically, men suffered the most significant health problems as a result of their drinking. This chapter will give you a quick overview of how things have changed for women drinking alcohol in modern times and some of the issues that have arisen as a result.

The surge of illegal drug use in the 1990s changed the shape of nightlife entertainment in western cultures when a new generation of young people began choosing to use drugs at dance music events. The movement away from drinking in traditional licensed establishments shocked the alcohol industry into rebranding and reinvigorating the alcohol market. New alcoholic drinks and venues such as wine bars were promoted to increase the appeal of alcohol to young people and women. Relaxed licensing restrictions made alcohol more readily available to purchase in supermarkets and corner shops. At the same time, women were finding themselves with more disposable income and greater cultural acceptance to drink alcohol in the same places and in the same manner as men.

Since the turn of the last millennium alcohol

industries have increasingly focused on selling their products to women, and the number of women developing relationships with alcohol has steadily grown. Drinks such as wine or gin are often portrayed to reflect different qualities to which women can aspire. Advertising shows us images of women drinking alcohol to deal with their stresses, celebrate successes or bond with their girlfriends, making alcohol seem like an indispensable part of every woman's life. Society has begun to reflect this change in women's drinking habits and reinforces similar messages about alcohol being essential to a woman's wellbeing.

Social pressure on women to drink alcohol is prevalent in the UK and Ireland, where I have previously been accused of 'rejecting my culture' when turning down a drink. If a woman chooses not to drink on social occasions, she may attract attention and is sometimes presumed to be pregnant depending on her age. While often encouraged to drink alcohol in much the same way as men, women will attract more social stigma and shame when they experience problems related to their alcohol use. Judgements made about a woman's ability to manage her family or career when using alcohol are often more harsh and severe than men may attract in similar positions.

Despite government attempts to highlight the concerns of drinking alcohol and promoting safe alcohol use levels, we are bombarded by alternative messages on television and in social media with alcohol glorified as an antidote to every modern problem. While different societies have different cultural ideas around alcohol use, some countries such as the UK represent alcohol as an integral part of daily life, as seen by their major soap operas. Footage of heavy alcohol use in reality television is served up as the 'typical behaviour of young people' or as an acceptable coping strategy for our lives. Whether you are aware of it or not, you are likely experiencing alcohol marketing and subliminal messaging about alcohol multiple times a day.

As an experiment, pay attention to how often and in what context you hear alcohol discussed in your daily interactions with people at work, in your family, community or while watching television. You may be surprised by how often this occurs and how fondly people speak of alcohol, even when they have had a negative experience with their use. One reason for this is that both drinking alcohol and sharing negative stories about our nights out helps people to bond and gain common ground with others. Alcohol incidents like losing personal possessions or having stupid arguments are relatable because many people who drink alcohol experience similar situations. At the same time, such stories can serve to validate and promote excessive alcohol use, make us feel better about our own behaviour and can ultimately prolong alcohol problems for longer than desirable.

 Listen out for the stories you hear in your life- do they serve to validate heavy alcohol use or are they more balanced? How do the stories fit with your own experiences of using alcohol? How do you feel your own culture, family and community influence your drinking behaviour?

Women and alcohol.

With more women drinking alcohol, there has been an increase in women having problems with alcohol. The gap between men and women experiencing issues with their drinking has been closing over the last 30 years globally with some British and Irish women now matching their male counterparts in their average weekly alcohol consumption. Unfortunately for women, the physical impact of alcohol use can be more severe than with men given the differences in body type between the sexes. Women tend to feel the effects of drinking quicker and typically achieve higher blood alcohol content readings than men will after consuming the same volume of alcohol. For many different reasons, women can suffer from negative physical consequences more quickly than men do when drinking similar amounts over time. This added vulnerability has resulted in a rise in women from their 20's developing and dying from alcohol-related organ failure, something almost unheard of 30 years ago. The health implications of excessive alcohol use will be discussed in greater detail within Chapter 3.

A further unwanted aspect of more women having problems with alcohol can be the knock-on impact this can have on families and children. It can be very stressful for children, young people or other adults living in families where a person has some problems with their drinking. Traditionally, addiction treatment services have solely focused on the person having the issue in the belief that if only this person stops drinking, then family life will fall back into place. While this may be true, it neglects the many families who are struggling with someone who is not currently considering changing their habits. Nor does this attitude help to address the trauma a person's drinking may have already caused to their family members. There is more recognition today that all family members who are affected by another person's drinking should be offered support regardless of their loved one attending alcohol treatment. Many children and young people are suffering needlessly in silence when there is support often available that can help them understand and be able to cope better with a parent's drinking. Information on how to minimise the impact of alcohol on your family is discussed further in Chapter 8 with extra resources found on my website.

Research continues to highlight the range of negative consequences which alcohol use can have in the development of unborn babies. Children affected by their mother drinking alcohol while they were in the womb may be diagnosed with foetal alcohol syndrome (FAS) or foetal alcohol spectrum disorder (FASD). Children born with these conditions may not develop as quickly as might be expected of a child the same age and can experience chronic health, behavioural and learning problems as they get older. The amount of alcohol required to harm a foetus in this way is not well known, which is why the general recommendation is for women to stop all use of alcohol during pregnancy. Limiting your alcohol use when you are thinking of getting pregnant is recommended as alcohol use can impact on a woman's fertility and her chances of conceiving. Considering the harmful impact alcohol can pose to a growing foetus, it would be wise to think about alcohol use or contraception options if there is a risk of having an unplanned pregnancy.

Despite the problems women can have with their alcohol use, and the higher levels of alcohol consumption among women globally, many women will never ask for support with their drinking, or they may wait until it is very late in the stage of helping. There are many reasons for this, being responsible for children is often a critical issue, not finding local alcohol support services approachable as a woman or simply through not wishing to be stigmatised and labelled as someone in need of alcohol support. Some women may not seek help sooner because they don't recognise their use of alcohol as being problematic. Perhaps they believe that only people who drink spirits have problems with alcohol and they only drink wine, or maybe they belong to a social circle where heavy consumption of alcohol has become an integrated part of life.

Alcohol culture and women.

As it has become more customary for women to drink, many have become entangled with alcohol in different ways. Often women begin drinking heavily when they first gain their independence from their families, while studying at university, travelling or working in a different place, or when they first move away from home. As we know, alcohol can serve very well for helping us to get along with other people and is used by many for dealing with the stresses in life. This can be a high-risk time for alcohol problems developing however, if people feel isolated from others or dislocated from their family or familiar community. People may come to rely heavily on alcohol to deal with their loneliness as well through enjoying their newly found freedoms. Women may develop a habit of heavy drinking during an earlier lifestyle yet find that this continues for one reason or another for many years. Other women may begin drinking more heavily in later years as a response to trauma or loss they have experienced or maybe by meeting a new partner who drinks heavily or through some other circumstance. However the relationship with alcohol began, excessive use can start taking a toll on a person's life and health over time when weeks become months and months become years.

Women who enter certain professions, particularly careers which are high-pressured or within typically male-dominated environments, may also be susceptible to heavy drinking either as an expectation of their jobs or as a way of dealing with constant high levels of stress. Given that a woman may work in her career for 30 years + this is a long time to be drinking at high levels, never mind the repeated stress levels endured otherwise.

Despite what we may be led to believe by parts of the media, people with higher disposable incomes consume substantially more alcohol (and use more drugs generally) than people on low incomes. The more readily available alcohol is (because it is more affordable), the more it is consumed. Any person leading a stressful life is more susceptible to using alcohol heavily as a means of coping with an impracticable life. High levels of stress also account for why adults who are parents typically report higher levels of drinking than adults who are not looking after children. Reducing the level of stress you experience in life is one of the best ways you can indirectly reduce your alcohol use and is a subject which we will return to throughout this book.

For many people, alcohol performs a variety of functions in their lives, whether it be enhancing social occasions or bonding, celebrating events or by marking the end of a working day or week. While there is nothing wrong with using alcohol for such purposes, it is crucial to understand the impact alcohol may be having on your own life and take responsibility to reduce the potential for experiencing negative consequences.

CHAPTER TWO: WHY WOMEN DRINK

Why drink?

There are multitudes of theories which attempt to answer the critical questions of why people start using alcohol, why some of them develop alcohol problems, and why many individuals struggle to change their drinking patterns.

Such theories include:

> biological explanations- that some people develop problems because they have inherited genetics from their families, making them more likely to drink excessively.

➢ psychological explanations- that some people use alcohol to cope with a personal issue such as social anxiety, depression, ADHD or trauma.

➢ sociological explanations- that some people use alcohol to help them deal with their life circumstances or because they belong to a group of heavy drinkers.

While these theories are fascinating, for this book to remain brief, this chapter will focus on some commonly reported reasons for women to drink alcohol, along with various practical solutions. Alcohol use plays so many diverse roles in our society with many people having different reasons for their drinking. Sometimes these reasons are what keep people drinking, long past when they know it has stopped being quite as much fun. If you feel you can relate to these reasons, it would be helpful for you to focus on improving this area when wishing to mend your relationship with alcohol.

Sleep and relaxation

One of the key reasons why women may use alcohol is to help them get off to sleep at night or to help relax after a long or busy day. Alcohol is often used in this way due to the relaxant effect it has on our nervous systems, slowing down our heart rate, breathing and thought processing. Our bodies feel increasingly relaxed as we consume more alcohol, in a similar way to how an anaesthetic feels, as will be discussed more in the next chapter. Drinking can deliver sleep and relaxation quickly when living busy and stressful lives, but as you will know if this is you, it can often come at a cost. The impact of a disrupted night's rest along with your body working hard to remove alcohol toxins can leave you feeling more tired than hoped in the mornings. Over time you may find yourself dreading the occasions you do not have alcohol available before bedtime knowing the difficulty in getting to sleep and so drinking becomes an increasingly required activity in the evenings.

One antidote to needing alcohol for sleep and

relaxation is to slow down and allow our bodies and minds the time to unwind and relax naturally after a working day. Try to include relaxing activities into your evenings which does not involve looking at a television, computer or mobile phone screen. While we may enjoy catching up with our favourite shows in the evening, spending too much 'screen time' as our means of leisure is one reason why we find it so challenging to relax and switch off our minds at the end of a busy day. Television is produced to keep our minds engaged, to absorb our senses so we do not notice the time passing or have the time to think about much else. Finding ourselves with no leisure time available to enjoy and unwind at the end of a day or week can be even more damaging to our emotional wellbeing and another primary contributor to insomnia. Many times, when we do finally switch off our devices or suddenly stop after a busy day, there will be a multitude of things going on in our heads. Thoughts and memories that we have avoided all day have the potential to keep us awake for hours to come.

Everyone is different and will find different things relaxing. Some people find arts and craft activities useful; for others, they might enjoy music, singing or dancing. Whether you're into reading, walking the dog, going to the gym, crosswords, DIY projects, baking or meeting up and having a laugh with friends- make sure you set aside time to do some activities in the evenings to help you relax where possible. Activities such as learning meditation and practising yoga are well established as helping promote relaxation and sleep along with a range of other positive benefits for our mood and wellbeing. Attending a class in your local area may be a good option for you if wanting to find new ways to spend your time. You can also learn basic techniques and follow guided instructions in online videos or checking through the resources on my website. Listening to relaxing meditations or music while going to sleep can also be helpful for you to help clear your mind if this is something you feel prevents you from sleep.

Things known to make it more difficult to sleep at night are drinking too much caffeine during the day and using brightly lit screens that trick our brains into thinking it is daytime. Therefore, be mindful of having too much tea or coffee during the day and try to spend an hour or two away from your phone/ television/ computer screen time before bed if possible.

Stress and escapism

Many people in this modern life experience stress, but women particularly feel it for several reasons that will be discussed as we continue this chapter. Our lives are more stressful in modern times than they have ever been in recent history. A recent survey commissioned by the Mental Health Foundation found that 81% of British Women had felt overwhelmed or unable to cope at some point in the previous year. Just as alcohol can provide quick relief to our troubles, it brings with it many of the issues we have discussed already. The problem with living a stressful life is that it produces harmful hormones in the body, the effects of which accumulate over time. It is easy to get caught in the trap of a strenuous lifestyle as we often believe that we can manage it in the short term until some point in the future when life improves. Unfortunately, this attitude has resulted in many people living with high levels of stress for most of their adult lives in the hope of enjoying life in retirement. We all know individuals who did not win at this gamble and so it is imperative to take measures to reduce your stress levels now and enjoy your life presently.

Alcohol use, while helping to forget a stressful day can also take our minds off doing what may be necessary to alleviate our worries, allowing the cycle to continue for longer than is healthy. When used in this way, alcohol can often become another hassle in your life despite the continued belief that it is helping us to deal with life's problems. For some people, their lives seem barely manageable, let alone without alcohol to cope. If this relates to your life, then you will need to think about some serious changes to reduce your stress levels before considering long term changes to your alcohol use. Are there ways in which you can take on fewer responsibilities in your life or reduce your stress in other ways? If there are things you have been putting off that you know need to be addressed to reduce your stress levels, then it is better to find a way of doing so than to continue using alcohol for this purpose.

If there is no way of reducing the stress you are experiencing in life, then it is advisable to learn new ways of responding to the tensions in your life and prioritise time for relaxing activities whenever possible. Often it can help to speak with friends or professionals for support when we are feeling overwhelmed. Don't be afraid of reaching out to others for help with your alcohol use or with any other areas of your life where you may be struggling. Counselling and therapy services may be helpful to you if you feel you need to learn new ways of responding to something that is troubling you. Alternatively, using time you may get to yourself wisely for relaxing activities such as having a back massage, sharing coffee with a best friend or planning a home-pampering spa session may be just as beneficial. Working on reducing other stressful factors in your life before changing your alcohol use can prove helpful for maintaining changes.

Loneliness and boredom.

Many people use alcohol to cope with loneliness and boredom they may feel in their lives just as we have covered how people may use alcohol for relaxation or to manage stress. Loneliness and boredom can manifest in women's lives for many reasons- perhaps you focused more energy on your career than you have on your relationships for years or you haven't found your match in life to start your own family yet. Maybe your family has grown up now, and you have more time and fewer responsibilities on your hands as you once had, or perhaps you feel misunderstood by the people around you and dissatisfied with the life you are currently living. As with all these reasons for drinking, unless you deal with the underlying issues you may be experiencing, then you are less likely to be able to manage your alcohol differently long term. Try and find other activities to enjoy or ways in which you may be able to replace the feeling of lacking you are experiencing. When we slow down and listen to ourselves, we may learn what it is we need in our lives to help us to experience 'wholeness' rather than an emptiness filled with alcohol. You will find a more in-depth discussion around this in the book's final chapter, Alcohol and Spirituality, and the resource sections on my website.

Trauma, loss and adverse childhood experiences

Lots of people in life, including many women, carry reminders of trauma with them daily. Some experiences are so severe they can cause physical or psychological damage that can last a lifetime. Traumatic events may occur together or can continue over time and often leave a profound psychological impact on an individual's beliefs about themselves and their place in the world. Experiences of abuse or neglect, especially events which happened during childhood, and particularly through experiencing sexual abuse, can influence many aspects of a person's life, not least how they use alcohol and other drugs.

Traumatic events need not have happened to us personally to experience post-traumatic stress disorder (PTSD). Witnessing traumatic experiences happening to others can also have an impact on our mental health. There is an increasing amount of research into how people who have experienced multiple traumatic events in their childhood may develop alcohol problems in their adult life. You can find more information about this research by searching for 'adverse childhood experiences' or following the links from my website.

Alcohol, like other drugs, can help to block bad memories and unfavourable life situations from our minds. With our culturally shared acceptance of alcohol's problem-solving abilities, we can often find encouragement and the companionship to 'drink our sorrows away'. As with the advice throughout this chapter, unless you learn new ways of dealing with the experiences you have had, then you will likely continue to use alcohol in the same way as part of your coping strategy. If you are serious about making long term changes to your alcohol use, trauma is something you must learn how to live with to have a healthier relationship with alcohol. You may find Chapters 9 and 10 in this book beneficial for learning new coping strategies and ways of relating to past trauma in your life, or you might wish to discuss any concerns with a professional. You can find links to professional services in your area on my website.

Caring for others.

Women make up the vast majority of official and unofficial carers in this world. Whether this involves caring for children, grandchildren, elderly parents or others in their families who need support, it is often women who are behind the scenes keeping everything going. How a woman manages with this responsibility relies on many things, not least the amount of support she has for the job but also on how she feels about this responsibility and other stress she may be dealing with in life.

When caring for others, it is even more important to schedule and prioritise time for yourself. The burnout rate of carers is immense because the pressure experienced in caring must be released somehow. Many carers keep going in fear of taking any time out from their responsibilities, not realising that time out is essential and will eventually happen whether this is planned or occurs unexpectedly. Finding support with other people who have similar caring responsibilities can be highly beneficial. Often there is professional or government support available offering respite care to families in recognition of the magnitude of challenges which carers can experience.

Drinking alcohol with another person.

Sharing your relationship with alcohol alongside another person can prove more challenging to make meaningful changes in your consumption unless the person you are drinking with also intends to make efforts in the same direction. When people make joint decisions about changing their drinking habits, they may find one another as a source of support, useful in making lifestyle changes together. As you will understand when reading Chapter 5, people are not always ready for change at the same time, and there remains a potential for one person to hold the other back when they cannot maintain changes as smoothly.

Drinking with others close to us, especially an intimate partner, can help to perpetuate your relationship with alcohol. Over time our close relationships develop shared rules and understandings that can help us to feel safe within our connection as we 'know where we stand'. Shared agreements about features of a relationship, such as when, where, and how we drink, can cause distress to either party when it comes to making changes. Questions naturally arise concerning how the relationship will change because of newly instated arrangements. While not impossible, changing your relationship with alcohol when you spend a lot of time with another drinker may require extra planning and preparation for how any changes affect others.

General dissatisfaction with life, career and being a woman in a man's world...

Henry David Thoreau once said that "the mass of men live lives of quiet desperation" and women can especially feel a general dissatisfaction with their lives for a great variety of reasons. Women often get a raw deal in life. Women generally need to work harder than men to gain recognition in their careers yet continue to be paid less than men in many equivalent roles.

Oftentimes, women are expected to be everything to all people- to have the ability to manage her career, to be dutiful daughters, mothers, wives and carers, let alone the myriad of ways in which women are exploited daily around the world. This book is written not to judge or criticise women in any way for how their relationship with alcohol may have developed. Instead, it aims to help women reduce their stress levels and increase their feelings of wholeness and connection which they can experience naturally in life, as a method to managing their alcohol intake.

Modern capitalist society is built upon making us feel dissatisfied with life. Advertising works by driving home to us how we need to buy more, spend more and consume more for us to be happy and fulfilled. Alcohol industries grow progressively more influential as we accept alcohol as a fast-fix antidote to modern life and increasingly base our lifestyles, relationships and identities on the alcoholic drinks which we consume.

Corporations swindle us by selling promises of love, fulfilment and happiness if we keep spending money on the latest things and participating in the latest crazes.

The remainder of this book will outline some ways we may step back from this trend and learn how we can improve our emotional wellbeing in a meaningful way. When we increase our satisfaction and acceptance of ourselves and our lives, external factors like advertising and other people's opinions will not affect our moods and behaviour in quite the same manner and our relationship with alcohol improves naturally.

FIONA STEELE

CHAPTER THREE: ALCOHOL 101

How much is too much alcohol?

While people may develop issues with any amount of alcohol taken, there are health promotion guidelines issued by many countries relating to the amounts believed to constitute safer use of alcohol. Broadly speaking, the higher the amount of alcohol consumed with the most frequency, the more significant the impact on our health. Most health promotion guidance suggests having 2- 3 days a week in which you do not drink alcohol and spreading the recommended weekly limit in smaller quantities throughout the week rather than drinking your weekly recommended limit in one session. General recommendations for women are to have no more than 1- 2 drinks per day or 2- 3 units of alcohol, as shall be explained below.

In the UK, we understand alcohol in terms of alcohol units. One unit of alcohol is the equivalent of 10ml of pure ethanol. Units of alcohol are useful to know because our bodies can process approximately one unit of alcohol per hour after you stop drinking*. If you need to know when you are clear of alcohol so you can drive a car or resume other responsibilities- calculate how many units you have consumed and leave the same number of hours from when you stop drinking. (*Some people may take longer than an hour to process one unit, for example, if they have an impaired liver or other underlying health condition).

Many drinks in the UK now have labelling to show how many units are in a container, but you can work this out yourself using the following multiplication.

Drink size in ml   X   Alcohol content %

$$\overline{}$$

1000

So therefore,

- A bottle of wine - 750ml @ 12% = 9 units

  (750 x 12 = 9,000 / 1000 = 9 units)

- A 500ml can of beer - 500ml @ 5% = 2.5 units

  (500 x 5 = 2,500 / 1000 = 2.5 units)

- A measure* of spirits - 25ml @ 40% = 1 unit

  (25 x 40 = 1000 / 1000 = 1 unit)

Be aware that standard spirit measures differ in places and especially when pouring at home - use a measure when drinking spirits so you know how much you are using, especially if using a drink diary or log.

In America, alcohol quantities are measured in terms of standard drinks. Each standard drink is roughly 1 ¾ UK units. The following image represents what is thought of as one standard drink in the USA.

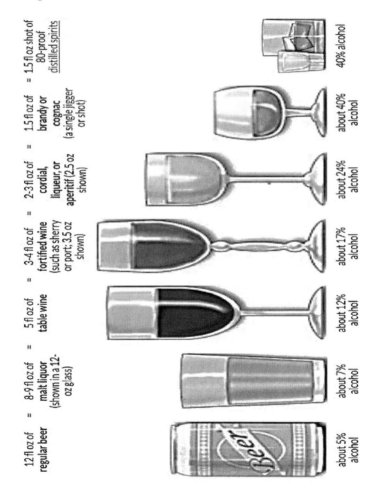

= 1.5 fl oz shot of 80-proof distilled spirits — 40% alcohol

= 1.5 fl oz of brandy or cognac (a single jigger or shot) — about 40% alcohol

= 2-3 fl oz of cordial, liqueur, or aperitif (2.5 oz shown) — about 24% alcohol

= 3-4 fl oz of fortified wine (such as sherry or port; 3.5 oz shown) — about 17% alcohol

= 5 fl oz of table wine — about 12% alcohol

= 8-9 fl oz of malt liquor (shown in a 12-oz glass) — about 7% alcohol

12 fl oz of regular beer — about 5% alcohol

The World Health Organisation issues guidance on what constitutes safer and riskier use of alcohol in terms of the amount of alcohol consumed.

Using the charts below, you can add up the scores relating to your drinking and check what the health risks are concerning how much alcohol you drink.

TABLE ONE:

Questions	Score					Your Score
	0	1	2	3	4	
How often do you have a drink containing alcohol?	Never	Monthly or less	2-4 times a month	2-3 times per week	4+ times per week	4 —
How many drinks* containing alcohol do you have on a typical day when drinking?	1-2	3-4	5-6	7-9	10+	1 —

Score	0	1	2	3	4	Your score
How often have you had six or more drinks* on a single occasion in the last year?	Never	Less than monthly	Monthly	Weekly	Daily or almost daily	2 ⑦

It doesn't matter if you prefer to score using drinks or alcohol units, just use the same measurements in repeated scoring.

Scores ranging from 0 – 3 are considered low risk, and there is no need to answer any further questions.

If you have scored higher than 3, you may continue to answer the items contained in Table Two over the next pages to determine the impact alcohol use may be having on your life.

TABLE TWO:

Questions	Score					Your Score
	0	1	2	3	4	
How often during the last six months have you been unable to stop drinking once you had started?	Never	Less than monthly	Monthly	Weekly	Daily or almost daily	3 —
How often during the last six months have you failed to do what was expected from you because of your drinking?	Never	Less than monthly	Monthly	Weekly	Daily or almost daily	1 —

Score	0	1	2	3	4	Your Score
How often during the last six months have you needed an alcoholic drink in the morning to get yourself going after a heavy drinking session?	Never	Less than monthly	Monthly	Weekly	Daily or almost daily	*0*
How often during the last six months have you felt guilt or remorse after drinking?	Never	Less than monthly	Monthly	Weekly	Daily or almost daily	*2*

How often during the last six months have you been unable to remember what happened the night before because you had been drinking?	Never	Less than monthly	Monthly	Weekly	Daily or almost daily	
						1
Have you or somebody else been injured as a result of your drinking?	Never	Less than monthly	Monthly	Weekly	Daily or almost daily	0
Has a relative or doctor been concerned about your drinking or suggested that you - cut down?	Never	Less than monthly	Monthly	Weekly	Daily or almost daily	1
						8

Score from Table 1 -> __7__ +

Score from Table 2 -> __8__

= Total score -> __15__

By adding up your total score, you can find out how risky your alcohol use is considered currently.

> ➤ 0-7: Low risk – While there are no completely safe levels of alcohol, the amount you drink is low risk.

> ⊘ 8- 15: Hazardous – Your drinking is putting you at increased risk of harm, including damage to your physical and mental health.

> ➤ 16-19: Higher risk – Drinking at this level will result in damage to your physical and mental health. You are also at risk of being alcohol dependent.

> ➤ 20+: Highest risk – Your drinking is seriously harming you, and you are likely to be alcohol dependent.

[WHO, Alcohol Use Disorder Identification Test].

Keep a note of your score if you plan to start making changes to your alcohol use. Nobody else needs to know this score, but if you come back to these questions in a few months from now, you can see how your score may have changed with your efforts.

Small regular rewards and recognition of any changes made are proven to help in changing habits over time. As we go through the book, you will learn many new ways in which you can reduce this score, and the overall impact alcohol may be having on your life currently.

The impact of alcohol on the body and emotions.

Alcohol can affect many different areas of your life, including your mental and physical health. Alcohol is processed by the body as a toxin, to be broken down and excreted with other toxins you accumulate in daily life. Excess drinking over time may cause a range of issues indicating poor general health including low energy levels, inability to concentrate, poor skin complexion and excess weight. The more alcohol or, the more regularly it is taken, the more pressure there will be on your organs, and this is one way in which the ill effects of taking too much alcohol can start to show. Your liver, pancreas and kidneys work to break down and excrete impurities. Regular alcohol use can cause inflammation of the liver leading to a build-up of toxins in the body which leave you feeling tired and run down in the short term and put you at risk of developing cirrhosis of the liver over a longer time frame. Unfortunately, female drinkers can find they start to develop problems with their health sooner than men would when engaging in the same style of drinking.

Over the longer term, the brain can also be affected in several ways. One way is that alcohol interferes with the body's uptake of necessary vitamins which over time can cause issues of malnutrition. The brain, deprived of all the materials it needs to be healthy, then also must endure successive bouts of dehydration which, combined over time, can lead to alcohol-related brain damage resulting in dementia type symptoms. These conditions are called Wernicke's Encephalopathy, the first stage which is potentially reversible if the person can stop their alcohol intake and increase their nutrition, and Korsakoff Syndrome, the end stage of accumulated brain damage which is no longer reversible. Vitamins such as Thiamine (Vitamin B1) can be prescribed to try and prevent the damage caused by drinking excess alcohol over time. Ensuring that you eat a healthy balanced diet is always essential, especially when using alcohol regularly. It may, however, be worth considering taking a supplement that includes Vitamin B1 if you are concerned about your alcohol intake due to alcohol's interference with how well our bodies absorb vitamins.

Our mental health can suffer significantly with excessive alcohol use over time. The constant pressure on the body to break down the toxins of alcohol can leave us feeling low in mood and motivation. Our sleep is affected, and any rest is often broken and disturbed. Sometimes, we may wake up after drinking wondering what exactly happened the previous evening, who we may have spoken to inappropriately and spend the rest of the day processing any other uncharacteristic choices or behaviours we might remember. The harmful impact alcohol can have on us accumulates over time, physically and mentally. Where drinking often begins in life as a fun pastime, it can start taking a heavy toll on a person's life as they get older and a few years of drinking alcohol has become ten, twenty, thirty years or more.

Alcohol as a drug.

Alcohol is a drug contained within alcoholic drinks which is often consumed by people to feel more relaxed, to loosen up socially, mark special occasions or help them to forget a stressful day. Alcohol is chemically related to ether, a drug which was widely used as an anaesthetic until it gathered too many safety concerns.

You may have guessed this already as using more substantial amounts of alcohol often makes us feel sleepy, affects our memory and coordination, and we may react uncharacteristically to people and situations- all typical symptoms of anaesthesia.

Alcohol belongs to a group of drugs called 'depressants' due to the depressant action they have upon our central nervous system. Our central nervous system is responsible for our brains sending signals to other parts of our bodies. This group of drugs slows down the reactions of the central nervous system explaining our slurred speech, poor coordination and slower reaction times generally. When we drink too much alcohol our bodies will often attempt to remove some by vomiting or may give other signals of nausea or sleepiness designed to stop us from drinking more alcohol. Serious problems can arise when people consume excessive amounts of alcohol, but the potential for complications increase when another drug is used along with drinking.

Using alcohol alongside other depressant drugs is responsible for many overdose deaths around the world. Other depressant drugs include many of the prescription drugs available for anxiety, pain or to aid sleep- benzodiazepines such as diazepam (Valium), Xanax, temazepam or Ativan and pain-relievers such as codeine, morphine, Vicodin, Tramadol, oxycodone among many others. When these drugs are used with alcohol, there is a significant increase to the depressant action on the central nervous system, and this can easily lead to an array of unwanted side effects occurring, including brain damage and death. Great care should be taken if you are using any of these medications as some

can stay in your system for many hours so even using some medicines in the morning may still impact on alcohol use that evening.

Alcohol can react with many different prescribed medications, not just the anti-anxiety and pain-relieving medications listed above. Always take a cautious approach when using alcohol with all medicines, including antidepressants, antibiotics, allergy, epilepsy and heart tablets. Read the medication guidance leaflet supplied with your prescription and check with your doctor if you are unsure about using medications with alcohol.

When alcohol is taken with stimulant drugs such as cocaine, amphetamines or even caffeine, the effect of these drugs often results in a person being able to consume much larger quantities of alcohol than they would otherwise. Stimulant drugs work to 'stimulate' or speed up the central nervous system, so reaction times quicken, the body feels more energised and processes such as your heart rate, breathing and speech all become faster. A significant impact of using stimulant drugs is the damage this can do to your heart. Heart damage can become a concern particularly for people who use alcohol and cocaine together as these form another drug when they react inside your body called cocaethylene. Using both alcohol and cocaine together is believed to be responsible for a growing number of heart attacks and deaths in people under the age of 40. In the short-term stimulant use can also cause palpitations, insomnia, mood swings, anxiety, panic attacks and seizures. Come down effects of stimulant drugs can significantly impact a person's mood and place them at a higher risk of depression, self-harm behaviours and suicide. Longer-term damage can also include erosion to the brain, heart failure, developing psychiatric conditions and a range of other harmful health and social consequences.

Other risk-taking behaviours.

Having issues controlling your intake of alcohol can also lead to other high-risk behaviours from occurring, for example, self-harming, considering the use of other drugs, such as cocaine, or engaging in risky sexual practices. Alcohol lowers our inhibitions which means we can behave and say things which are uncharacteristic for us because of our alcohol consumption. Usually, these risks will increase with the amount of alcohol taken, but sometimes only one drink is required for us to make a string of bad decisions.

If you know that drinking alcohol makes it more likely for you to engage in other harmful behaviours, then it may be even more crucial for you to focus your energies on learning new ways of managing your life. You may be able to prepare and safeguard against such behaviours, for example, by removing sharp objects from your environment if you can hurt yourself when you have been drinking. How to prepare for potential high-risk situations depends upon the particular risk. Thinking ahead may include ensuring you are not able to contact a drug dealer when you are drinking alcohol or always carrying condoms with you when drinking at social occasions. Unfortunately, some people may find that the only way to prevent these other behaviours from occurring is to stop drinking alcohol altogether.

The darker side of alcohol.

Alcohol has the ability to change people's personalities significantly and can bring out a darker side that may never appear when the person is not drinking. As alcohol loosens a person's inhibitions they can feel more lively and social but can also, especially when drinking in larger quantities, become more argumentative, aggressive and in some cases violent. Our society's love affair with alcohol can hide much darker secrets, not least that incidents of domestic violence are known to spike at times when large amounts of alcohol are typically consumed. Times of celebration such as Christmas, birthdays or during significant football matches or other sporting events can be scarred by heavy alcohol use when this results in violence or aggression. The risks of being both a victim and perpetrator of violence increase significantly at times and in spaces where people consume large amounts of alcohol.

Excessive alcohol use is often intertwined with sexual

assaults both through increasing the likelihood of a sexual assault happening and in dealing with the trauma left in the aftermath. The chances of a sexual assault taking place increase significantly when both perpetrators and victims have been drinking alcohol. Alcohol can cause people to behave in very uncharacteristic ways, and issues of consent can become sketchy when there is little recollection of the events leading up to and including sexual contact with another person. Using alcohol as a way of coping with the trauma of sexual violence can, unfortunately, place the woman at a higher risk of further sexual assaults occurring in her lifetime.

If abuse and violence are issues that affect you or someone you love, it may be time to consider how alcohol use contributes towards this and take immediate steps to reduce these experiences in your life. For more information and links to support services in your area, please refer to the resource section of my website, www.fionasteele.com

FIONA STEELE

CHAPTER FOUR:
ALCOHOL PROBLEMS

Terms used to describe alcohol problems.

There are different ways alcohol problems are labelled depending on how the person uses alcohol and whereabouts in the world it is being discussed. Addiction is a term used to describe a person who has lost control over their drinking, and it is harming an aspect of their life. Addiction can refer to a person who drinks daily and may be physically dependent on alcohol or to someone who drinks less frequently but in large quantities despite it negatively affecting their health, relationships or employment over a significant period.

'Alcohol dependence' and 'alcohol abuse' are terms often used in America, separating these two types of problematic drinkers into different categories. Alcohol dependence refers to the body's physical and psychological dependence on alcohol characterised by an uncontrollable urge to drink and often best describes people who drink daily. Alcohol abuse is used to describe binge drinking behaviour or when people drink far more alcohol than the daily recommended guidelines.

'Alcohol Use Disorder' is a more recent term used to describe the range of problems people can have when drinking alcohol. The disorder may be classed as mild, moderate or severe, depending on the number of matching criteria and the impact the person's alcohol use is having upon their life. Symptoms must be present for at least a year for an addiction or alcohol use disorder to be diagnosed.

'Alcoholism', 'addict' and 'alcoholic' are terms no longer preferred as they typically represent images of a person who is 'down and out' or living on the street in many people's imaginations. The stigma attached to these labels encourage us to fear others and feel like they are not to be trusted. These terms are therefore not helpful or relatable to most people experiencing alcohol problems. In the UK, we have also moved away from the label 'abuse' given the negative connotations of the word used in other ways and regularly use the term 'misuse' instead.

My usual preference is to talk about alcohol use and heavy alcohol use as a way of limiting the stigma this can attract from other people. I have seen how individuals can be treated differently by services, friends and even family members when given the label alcoholic. I have also witnessed how individuals can lose hope and motivation to change their alcohol use when they begin to internalise and subconsciously live up to these labels. We can all experience issues with drinking alcohol on occasions or at different times of our lives, branding some people as being different or unique from others I feel is unhelpful.

Checklist for assessing alcohol use problems.

Consider the following questions used for diagnosing problems with alcohol and think about how many you have experienced during the previous 12 months.

-> Have a strong desire or compulsion to use alcohol. This may include having had many failed attempts at cutting down or stopping alcohol use in the past.

-> Have difficulties controlling your use of alcohol by starting sooner in the day, drinking larger volumes or over a longer time frame than was intended.

-> Have experienced withdrawal symptoms after stopping using alcohol. These may range from reasonably mild to very serious depending on how much, how often and for how long a person has been drinking. Symptoms tend to peak around 24- 48 hours after stopping drinking, although they may continue for much longer depending on the seriousness of the person's alcohol dependence. Withdrawal symptoms can include shaking hands, fast heart rate, insomnia and low mood and are discussed in further detail below.

-> Have experienced increased tolerance, so you need to drink more alcohol to achieve the desired effects.

-> Time once spent enjoying other interests or recreational pursuits has shrunk because of alcohol use. In contrast, more time is spent obtaining alcohol, consuming alcohol or recovering from the effects of alcohol.

-> Alcohol use continues despite having a detrimental impact on a person's life. Consequences include developing health problems such as having impaired liver function, social issues such as becoming unemployed, arrested or homeless due to alcohol use, relationship or family breakdowns or any other significant problem caused by alcohol use.

A diagnosis of alcohol dependence will be made when three or more of these criteria have been present together during the previous year. Continuing to drink in this way will have a damaging impact on your life and wellbeing if it hasn't already. While this may have been a pattern you have repeated for some time, you will most likely know many ways your life will improve if you can limit your use of alcohol.

Abstinence goals or harm reduction.

When you are hoping to change your relationship with alcohol, there are many ways you can do this. Some people reach a point where they feel there are no positive reasons for them to continue drinking alcohol and know that, for them, they need to stop drinking altogether. Abstinence of alcohol, or not using alcohol at all, is a great goal to aim for, especially when alcohol is having a particularly negative impact on your life. Again, there are different ways to get to that point. Some people have the self-control to reduce their use of alcohol over a while, so they don't feel the impact of stopping suddenly. Other people may set a date in advance on which to make changes while other people may spontaneously declare that 'enough is enough' and have the coping strategies and support in their lives to follow this through.

It is worth thinking about what you wish to do about alcohol before you make any drastic changes in how you drink. If you regularly drink to excess, there may be a chance that you are physically reliant on alcohol and need to consider and prepare for any withdrawal symptoms you may experience as a result of stopping drinking. Such withdrawal symptoms can include hand tremors, insomnia, fever, nausea and anxiety to more severe issues such as hallucinations and seizures. There are medications available to ward off withdrawal symptoms, usually in the form of benzodiazepine tablets given in decreasing doses over several days to a week. The same process can be achieved by reducing alcohol intake over five days to a week or longer.

Detoxification from alcohol and the need for rehabilitation.

Some people may need to enter a residential facility for them to receive the required medical assistance for their withdrawal period. Cleansing the body from alcohol is referred to as an alcohol detox or detoxification process and can last from a few days up to a week or two. Hospital emergency rooms can sometimes help people experiencing alcohol withdrawal symptoms, given the potential for life-threatening issues in severe cases. Stabilising the person is usually done as quickly as possible, and the person may only receive the medication they need until they can meet with their general practitioner.

When a person has successfully detoxified from their alcohol withdrawal, they may then return home or spend another period completing alcohol rehabilitation. People often spend around 3- 6 months in the rehabilitation process, but some facilities may offer considerably more or less than this depending on where you live and your access to healthcare.

The positives of residential rehabilitation

-> It aims to provide a supportive environment in which you can learn new coping skills and develop support strategies to help you maintain new choices around alcohol going forward.

-> The environment and professionals on-site fully support the initial stages of abstinence. Difficulties in your home environment can be faced when feeling more clear-minded.

-> It offers structured education and counselling sessions, both 1 to 1 and within a group, that will help teach you about your relationship with alcohol and how any personal issues may be influencing your ability to change.

-> You will meet other people who are on a similar journey who you could find supportive when you leave the facility.

<u>The negatives of residential rehabilitation</u>

-> Often residential facilities are very expensive or otherwise difficult to access for many people due to a variety of issues- not located close to home, no options for childcare responsibilities, unable to take the time required away from work or home life etc.

-> It can create a false sense of security because the environment is so different from your own. Positive changes made in residential facilities may not be as easy to maintain on returning home. Keeping up changes following your stay is a difficult thing to practice without returning home so many rehab facilities will allow people back for short periods during their stay so they may prepare for the impact of finally leaving.

-> Some of the expectations of living in a residential facility may suit some people better than others. Many alcohol rehabilitation facilities are offered by religious institutions, perhaps requiring residents to participate in religious services during their stay. Facilities may have rules such as early morning starts, participating in group work sessions and other house rules which may not suit everybody.

-> While the relationships developed at residential rehabilitation facilities may be supportive in more structured environments, caution should be taken in these having a detrimental impact at any stage on leaving.

Rehabilitation completed in a residential environment can offer you new learning and insight into your drinking, which can prove helpful when changing your relationship with alcohol. If you can make changes to your alcohol use while remaining within your home environment, this is often more favourable given the more authentic conditions. There are so many things to consider when thinking about entering a period of rehabilitation, so you need to think carefully about the right decision for you. One thing to be aware of, however, is the temptation 'to hide' in rehab for a while without considering the real changes you will need to make in your life on leaving the facility.

Essentially, you cannot expect to change your relationship with alcohol on a long-term basis if you are not prepared to modify some aspects of your life to support this alteration. Lifestyle changes such as not associating with the same people, going to the same places and doing the same things as you associate with alcohol and how you spend your leisure time will all need to be analysed. Stopping your use of alcohol can require many changes to your lifestyle, whether you enter a residential rehabilitation facility, or you do not.

For people that are not yet ready to make such drastic changes in their lives or who may wish to continue their use of alcohol in a more controlled manner, there is a selection of helpful tips and advice in Chapter 6. For most people, lessening their alcohol intake in some way would be beneficial to them whether this is through small gradual steps or by pledging to complete a week or a month without alcohol. It is essential to make goals in your life achievable, so do not set a longer time frame for going without alcohol than you feel you can manage without too much discomfort. For some people, they may set a challenge to remain alcohol-free for one month so they may reassess their relationship with alcohol over some time, for others a day or a week may be a more reasonable goal currently.

Setting yourself goals to remain alcohol-free and then achieving them is a great way to begin to put a bit of distance between yourself and your drinking. Achieving goals gives us the confidence to continue, allows our body and mind to adjust to a new level of alcohol intake and provides us with some practice in learning new ways of coping and finding other ways to spend time. Setting goals such as- 'I'm not going to drink this evening/ weekend/ week' is much easier to process in our minds than 'I'm never going to drink again' or any other goal that seems too far away right now. The remainder of this book and the extra resources contained on my website will cover further advice and information on ways in which you may regain control over your alcohol use.

CHAPTER FIVE:
HOW CHANGE HAPPENS

Changing the way we use alcohol is similar to how we may change other behaviours in our lives, such as eating better, exercising more or stopping smoking. Changing behaviour is not often easy and can take time, especially when routines have been practised for many years. Sometimes people may wonder why somebody else 'simply does not stop drinking alcohol' however, may forget how difficult they have found new behaviour changes concerning something in their own life. The stages outlined below are relevant to any behaviour change, whether it be eating less chocolate or making more time for our loved ones. While changing habits will require some effort, many people will find ways that work for them with the right knowledge, preparation, support and attitude.

There are two fundamental ingredients when it comes to making changes in our life- our motivations for doing so and our confidence and belief in our ability to make positive changes.

These qualities would typically be assessed in an addiction service using a scale for answers from 1 – 10.

Q1. How motivated are you to change your behaviour
(i.e. drinking less or stopping alcohol use)?

1   2   3   4   (5)   6   7   8   9   10

Not motivated ~ Fairly motivated ~ Highly motivated

Q2. How confident are you in your ability to make changes to your drinking behaviour currently?

(1)   2   3   4   5   6   7   8   9   10

Not confident ~ Fairly confident ~ Highly confident

Think about your selected scores for motivation and confidence when answering the next questions-

Explain why you have scaled yourself on that number and not the number below?

> I enjoy alcohol and don't want to cut back. I never commit, alway lapse into old ways.

Outline the steps that would need to happen for you to scale yourself a number higher?

> Seeing positive changes eg weight loss, better mental health

Stages of Change.

When people are considering improving their behaviour, there are specific steps they go through that can be helpful to understand when hoping to make changes with alcohol. Through understanding how you, or someone else, may currently be feeling about changing drinking habits, it is easier to know how to proceed onto the next stage. Psychologists James Prochaska and Carlo DiClemente devised the following 'Stages of Change' that can be helpful to think about in relation to how most people can intentionally change their behaviour over time.

Pre-contemplation stage.

The stage of pre-contemplation means that the person is not thinking their behaviour poses a problem for them, and therefore, is not considering making any changes. Other people may believe that the person's behaviour, such as their drinking, is an issue. Still, until someone realises this for themselves, they will not begin to think about changing anything.

Someone may be nudged onto the next stage of contemplation and start to consider changes, but this can require a delicate balance of highlighting valid concerns to the person while trying to understand what using alcohol means for them. Blaming, criticising or attempting to change a person's thoughts to be more like your own, as typically happens, does nothing to help people achieve meaningful change.

When we feel criticised regarding our conduct, the natural reaction is to defend it. This response applies to many of our behaviours if you want to think about some other examples. People who experience problems with their drinking are usually well aware of what is good and what is not so good about this habit. When other people highlight the negatives of alcohol use, we may over-emphasise the positive qualities we obtain from drinking. Some people can remain stuck for many years in what seems like a position of denial about the impact of their alcohol use, but this may reflect their reaction to criticism rather than how they genuinely feel about their habits.

Asking somebody about what they find beneficial about their drinking and listening to what the person has to say before discussing any negative impact will likely provoke a more honest discussion about the person's experiences. When people feel that their opinions are valued and understood, they may become more open to considering any problems with their drinking. Discussing such topics with a sense of curiosity will allow you to learn much more about the person and why they drink rather than offering lectures based on condemnation and consequences.

Accurate assessment of your own alcohol use following the information and advice contained in this book should help you to understand what changes may be of benefit to you.

Contemplation.

The person is beginning to think that their behaviour may be causing some problems for them and is contemplating ways in which they might like to change things. Sometimes people arrive at this stage over time or through the influence of somebody else in their lives. At times people may suddenly begin to think about change when they reach a crisis point of some sort, for example, due to the diagnosis of a health problem or maybe with the aftershock of a particularly destructive drinking session. People may remain in the stage of thinking about changing for a short time or a long time, depending on their motivation and confidence for making changes.

Thinking about the pros and cons of changing alcohol use may be a beneficial exercise to complete at this stage, as outlined at the end of this chapter. Think about how your life will improve and what you could gain from changing your behaviour as well as what you are most concerned about. Writing things out on paper is always recommended so you can be clear on what you stand to gain and your personal concerns which require more focus. Fears about how your life may change or how you will manage without using alcohol can be planned for in order to build your confidence to move forward.

Preparation.

The person has decided to do something about their behaviour and will actively begin researching or planning how to make changes to their alcohol intake, perhaps by contacting an addiction service or discussing ideas with others. Using the information contained within this book, thinking about and preparing for how your life will change are valid ways to support yourself into the action stages.

Motivation and confidence hopefully increase at this time to enable us to move forward, or we may become stuck with the belief that we can't change. To help increase motivation it is useful to think about the current strengths in your life and reflect on changes you may have made previously with your alcohol use or when changing another habit like giving up smoking. What did you find worked for you on that occasion? Did you take up new habits or how did you change your mindset?

One of the worst things we can do for someone, and

particularly at this stage, is to tell them what they have to do or what we feel would be suitable for them. While this is often a response when people talk to others about their problems with alcohol, let's imagine a scenario where you have decided to improve your life, for example by eating less chocolate, joining a gym or losing weight. You've thought about what this change would mean to you, how you might go about it and when you might do it. Then someone in your life comes along and with the best of intentions says to you-

> "Do you know what you should do? You should eat less chocolate/ join a gym/ lose weight".

How would you feel about your life improvement plans then? Are you still as motivated to do it now somebody else might think it was their idea?

If someone close to you is preparing for making changes, we can support them by asking questions about why the decision is important to them and how they are thinking about going about it. Do not give the person advice on what you think they should or should not do at this stage unless specifically asked to do so!

Another human reaction we can possess is to lose interest in something when someone else seemingly takes over the direction and decisions needed for us to take action. When other people talk about changing their behaviour, it is essential to encourage their confidence and belief in their ability to make changes. Encouraging people to develop a strategy for how they will manage the necessary lifestyle changes and supporting their plans is a powerful way you may help. Try to resist thinking that your approach would be better or that you can somehow take the actions that are necessary on another person's behalf.

Action.

The person takes the first steps in changing their behaviour. Perhaps you have stopped drinking alcohol altogether, have cut down or controlled your alcohol use better in some way. While this stage is quite short-lived, it can be an emotional time. Withdrawal symptoms can occur, and fears may set in about the noticeable differences in your life. At the same time, you may feel good about the changes you have made and start to imagine a new identity that can incorporate these latest developments. If you have been using alcohol habitually, it may take some time for your brain to catch up with any changes, and this can result in mood swings or issues with eating, sleeping and concentration. Remember that withdrawal symptoms can be physically dangerous when somebody stops drinking suddenly, as discussed in the previous chapter. Most people should find that their symptoms will reduce after the first few days and their mood improves over the following week.

Any improvements towards a person's desired intentions with alcohol deserve to be recognised and rewarded. Smaller adjustments in the beginning may help to increase confidence in making further changes. More dramatic shifts in reducing alcohol use will require considerably more effort to initiate and maintain, however, can also bring superior rewards sooner which can increase feelings of motivation and the will to keep going.

Maintenance.

The person continues to maintain the changes they have made concerning their alcohol use. All the energy and jubilation of taking the first steps wears off, and people need to learn new ways of how to deal with a broad range of emotions without the support of their 'quick-fix friend'. The maintenance stage can be tough for people. Still, the more preparation, planning and energy you put into developing a new lifestyle that can support new choices, the higher your chances of success at remaining in this stage. Finding different ways of managing stressful situations is also essential to lessen the risk of using alcohol again for this purpose.

Think of making modifications in your life like a seesaw, where alcohol is removed something else needs to take its place, for example:

-> If you are spending less time and money on drink, what will you do now with your time and money?

-> If you were drinking with someone else, what will you do now with that person that does not involve alcohol or who will you associate yourself with if you see them less?

-> If you were drinking to help you with sleep, stress, boredom, trauma, loneliness, how will you deal with those things without using alcohol?

If you do not have satisfactory answers and action plans relating to these sorts of questions, your chances of maintaining any new drinking patterns will be more challenging. Further information about how to boost your chances of succeeding with long term changes is discussed more in Chapter 7. Worksheets and other resources to help you think through making changes are available to download from my website.

Relapse.

The person may return to their previous behaviour for a variety of reasons. If the person has a few drinks but stops the following day again this is referred to as a 'lapse'; when people return to their previous drinking for longer, it is called a 'relapse'. Relapse is considered as a normal and expected stage of modifying behaviour and can help us to learn better ways of maintaining changes we make in the future. While many people feel like they have failed altogether when they resume old habits, it is helpful to remember that some backwards and forwards is usual when it comes to changing our ways. Rather than beating yourself up, reflect upon what went well when you had made some changes and use what happened as a setback to readjust your plan for your next attempt.

It may take some time to mentally prepare before a person is ready to try making changes again. Still, we can best encourage their motivation by focusing on their strengths, what they did well, and help them to re-evaluate their own goals and strategies.

Benefits noticed when reducing alcohol intake

There are many benefits you may observe when you reduce your use of alcohol. While sleep may be affected initially, your quality of sleep will likely improve after the first week, leaving you feeling less tired and more able to concentrate. Your liver and other organs are more able to recover and resume normal functioning, also contributing to you starting to feel better with more energy. You may notice an improvement in your weight from the reduced calorie intake and your skin will improve from being better hydrated. The longer you can stay away from alcohol, the less likely you will experience illnesses related to alcohol, heart attacks, stroke and certain cancers.

Other benefits may include having more money, feeling less embarrassed by any drunken behaviours, less likely to upset your family and friends, less likely to have an accident or get into other harmful situations. When we combine reductions in alcohol use with other healthy activities such as increasing exercise or finding new hobbies, then this may bring even further benefits and improvements to our physical health and emotional wellbeing.

Decisional Balance Exercise

Thinking about the reasons people have for and against changing their relationship with alcohol can help to move people forward with these outlined stages of change. Take some time to think about how you would answer the following questions.

When you finish, you will have gained insight into your personal motivations regarding changing your drinking habits and better understand what is holding you back from attempting and achieving lifestyle adjustments.

How might my life change for the better if I reduced or stopped my alcohol use?	How might my life change for the worse if I reduced or stopped my alcohol use?
What would I notice immediately?	What would I notice immediately?
Better sleep, No hangovers	Less joy.
What would I notice after a while?	What would I notice after a while?
Weight loss. More money.	

FIONA STEELE

CHAPTER SIX:
THE ACTION PLAN

However you would like to continue your relationship with alcohol, thorough preparation is your key to success. Planning for changes makes sense when you think about how you might prepare meal ideas and shop for healthy foods if you are intending on changing your diet the following week or perhaps you have packed your gym outfit for the next day to increase your chances of exercising. Adjusting your relationship with alcohol also takes preparation, so this chapter will give you an overview of what to think about when considering changing your habits.

Reducing the harms associated with alcohol.

Harm reduction strategies can be useful if you're currently not ready to cut down or stop drinking alcohol. There are various ways you can reduce the risks associated with your alcohol use, depending on how you currently drink. Whether you use alcohol every day or more occasionally, there are probably some strategies you can implement to make your use of alcohol safer for you and more enjoyable.

Many people around the world enjoy the customary use of alcohol. Alcohol is often consumed with meals, for example, and there is nothing necessarily wrong with regularly drinking small quantities. Problems may arise related to consistent use if it negatively impacts the person's health, relationships, finances, or in other ways. Most health promotion advice would suggest that it is best to have a few days a week when we do not drink alcohol to allow our bodies time to recover. Another reason to try and leave days between drinking alcohol is that drinking on most days can slide into a person feeling more dependent on alcohol, and it becomes a more difficult habit to break with time.

Understanding how much you are drinking is critical. Keep a log of every drink you have on a given day when possible. Nobody else needs to see this log, but it is useful for you to know how much you are drinking on a daily and weekly basis. The act of recording your drink intake can sometimes be enough to change your habits if you have not been consciously noting your drinks previously. If you wish to step down on how much you are drinking your log will prove useful. Try to remain mindful of how many drinks you are having, how many you intended to have, and how this worked out for you. You may notice a pattern to your drinking that can bring more awareness to how you can limit your alcohol use at high-risk times.

Pacing yourself while drinking is also vital if you want to be able to control the onset of drunkenness, limit the possibilities of 'blacking out' or other memory loss and if you wish to resume a healthier relationship with alcohol. Take a note of the time you poured your last drink and how long you take to drink it. Smaller sips or shorter gulps can help you to drink more slowly, and if you can extend the time between your drinks, this can help you control the pace better. A glass of water or a soft drink between alcoholic beverages will help you stay hydrated and limit your hangover the next day. Starting to drink later in the day can also limit how much alcohol you consume overall.

Set yourself up for keeping your intentions regarding your use of alcohol by thinking about how much alcohol you have available to you. If you are in the house, only purchase the amount of alcohol which you would like to drink that day if you find yourself using more than you previously intended. Think about buying smaller bottles than usual and stay away from offers promising more than you need. It may cost you slightly more initially, however drinking less will help you to spend less money overall. Having a selection of alcohol-free drinks at hand can help if you find yourself using alcohol when you are thirsty.

If you drink away from home in entertainment spaces then plan how much money you take with you, maybe leave your bank card at home if this is possible. Buying your own drinks rather than participating in buying 'rounds' can also help you to drink at your own pace. It is customary in many European countries to leave time between finishing a drink and ordering the next one whereas often in the UK people will order the next drink before finishing the one they have. This slight change in perspective, in slowing down and savouring your glass rather than rushing ahead to get the next one, and then the next one, would help many British people limit the harmful effects of drinking alcohol.

Drinking a drink that has less alcohol in it can be useful if you find it difficult to pace yourself using the above tips. For example, using a spirit measure when pouring spirits such as vodka, gin or rum into your drinks will likely lead to having less alcohol content than a 'hand-poured' estimate. The same advice applies with glasses of wine or other beverages that come from a bottle. Drinking wine or beer that has less alcohol content or switching to another drink that has less alcohol can help limit how quickly you feel the effects of drinking and put less pressure on your body in breaking the alcohol down afterwards.

By looking after ourselves in other ways, we can also help to limit the impact alcohol can have on us. Think about how well-rested you are, your frame of mind and general stress levels before drinking and how much you have eaten or need to eat to limit the adverse effects alcohol may have on you on that occasion. Having food in our stomach can slow the impact of alcohol down. It will not make a difference to your blood alcohol content overall as you drink more, but it will help the effects to come on more slowly rather than all at once. Having adequate rest and a relaxed frame of mind will also help limit any unwanted effects from arising. For some people drinking alcohol can help to alleviate their tension, for other people, alcohol can amplify their stress, perhaps helping initially, but then the pressures can seem all the worse after having more drink.

Understanding triggers

Triggers to your alcohol use generally revolve around people, places and things. People in your life that you may need to be mindful of are those whom you consume alcohol with and the people who cause you stress which in turn, may weaken your resolve after seeing them. Planning is the paramount factor here. Make a list of the people who may influence your use of alcohol. Think about why this is and what you could do to lessen their sway upon you.

For example, if you tend to drink with particular people, think about how you would like those relationships to look like moving forward. Do you still want this person in your life? How might you be able to interact with them differently to lessen your use of alcohol? Some people may need to take a break from some of their friendships until they can learn how to manage alcohol use in their company. For other people, they may be able to continue their relationship by visiting coffee shops instead of bars or by meeting for brunch rather than dinner.

The people you know who cause you stress in your life may require a different kind of preparation. Is there a way of lessening the tension by talking about whatever it is you find difficult in the relationship? Can you change the way you relate to this person either practically or emotionally, to cause you less pain overall? Can you practice new ways of responding to stressful situations, so you don't use alcohol for this purpose?

You may find similar triggers exist for you with particular places. Maybe you use alcohol more when you return to a neighbourhood where you lived previously or somewhere you have made specific memories. Perhaps your alcohol use is connected to your career, college or even attending mother and baby parties. Anywhere which you associate with drinking and know you might find it difficult not to drink requires some thought about what you intend to do. Plan alternative drinks you can have, different places you can go and what you might tell people if they enquire why you are not drinking in the same way. Asking people not to offer you alcoholic drinks if you are at a party or function can also be useful if this is possible.

Situations and other things in your life which you associate with drinking will also require thinking about and planned for in much the same way. You may already know the special occasions when you will find it harder not to drink such as anniversaries, weddings or funerals so think about ways you might make this easier on yourself. Find companionship in people you know who do not drink or can support you in drinking less. Arrange to do something pleasurable for yourself in advance on difficult days if you can or anything else you can find to keep busy enough at difficult times so that your mind doesn't wander towards alcohol.

Alcohol, like other drugs, may be used in a way to block out our feelings or 'put our heads in the sand' about issues in our lives which we may not wish to confront. To increase your chances of success in changing your relationship to alcohol, think about and deal with any other issues you think alcohol might have been helping you to avoid. We have covered many of these in Chapter 2. Still, if there are other stresses in your life you haven't dealt with yet, they will likely keep resurfacing until you do something about them. Changing your use of alcohol will be more difficult if these are left unaddressed, or there is a risk that your drinking may morph into other unhealthy habits.

Setting rules and changing attitude

Setting rules for yourself is a valuable part of any strategy in managing alcohol in new ways. Practices might involve how many drinks you consume within a set time, deciding not to drink until after a specific time, on a given day or while in a particular place. Other rules might include not drinking a certain drink, not drinking while with your children or not drinking alone. Most people who drink alcohol have formed standards they adhere to, even people who drink frequently will likely have rules they try and keep.

Rules about drinking can also be culturally dictated, for example, it may be considered rude not to take alcohol for a toast at weddings, or it may be expected within a certain group of people to drink in a specific way. Many times, in the UK and Ireland, the aim of drinking is simply 'to get drunk'. Think about the practices you have around alcohol currently and how you might like to implement new rules. Interestingly, the rules we set ourselves in life are often associated with who we see ourselves as a person. College students, for instance, may not consider such strict guidelines for themselves as new parents might because their situations are very dissimilar with different responsibilities. How do your practices around alcohol fit with the way you see yourself or how you would like to see yourself? Maybe you developed your rules at a time when you had different responsibilities than you have now, and these need re-evaluated? How would you like to see yourself going forward, and what principles would this ideal version of ourselves have concerning drinking alcohol?

Remember that smaller steps often amount to more significant gains. If you are some way away from keeping rules that you would have ideally then practice with simpler ones that you can stick to along your way. It is much better to make a rule for yourself and stick to it for a while than it is for you to leap ahead and make unrealistic rules that you end up breaking. Start with setting yourself small intentions, for example, by deciding to start drinking later in the day than usual, having one less drink than you ordinarily would or aim to take a day, week or month away from drinking. Set yourself goals that you think you can stick to and build upon your successes rather than aiming too high and knocking your confidence. Plan rewards for yourself after your first day, week or after managing difficult situations better. Small rewards along the way are proven to help train your brain into forming new habits, will give you something to look forward to and help you to gain a sense of accomplishment on your journey.

FIONA STEELE

CHAPTER SEVEN: MAINTENANCE

When actions have been taken to change the nature of your drinking, and the initial 'honeymoon' stage of changing the behaviour wears off, the biggest challenge to people can be how to maintain such changes and cement them into a new lifestyle. It is always important to remember the reasons why you decided to make the changes, but sometimes the reasons people have initially may not be as relevant over time. Adopting a new lifestyle and changing the way you think about alcohol is fundamental to supporting desired changes over the longer term.

Changing our habits takes time and effort, and a person may attempt to make changes many times before they establish a new relationship with alcohol. Many different elements can support lasting changes in alcohol use and the more of these which feature in a person's life, the higher the likelihood of maintaining changes over time.

Self-regulation.

Any habit built up over time can be difficult to change because our brains integrate pathways for these habits into our subconscious minds becoming stronger over time. Cravings may appear this way, emerging from outside of our perception at any moment as a reminder of the brain pathways we have formed. Sometimes when people are trying very hard to change habits, they may feel panicked thinking they have unconsciously had a drink somehow, or they might have dreams about drinking. Cravings and anxiety about drinking will lessen as time goes on, and the brain begins to break down the pathways it has made for that habit. In the meantime, we require effort and awareness to regulate our thoughts and feelings, so they do not quickly spiral into a relapse. Think of it like being your parent, boss or alcohol counsellor and become conscious of when your brain is attempting to trick you back into drinking. Learning how to respond in a better way to destructive thoughts we may be having is covered in more detail in Chapter 9.

Active awareness of what you are thinking and feeling throughout the day and applying conscious effort to change any unhelpful thoughts about alcohol will help your brain to form new neural pathways which will support your new habits. Over time old pathways for drinking are broken down, and new habits will become more second nature for you. While this may sound like hard work (and it can be) the rewards for starting to gain control of the way you think is the key to your success in anything that you do in life.

Changing the way that you feel on a given day starts with changing how you think about your experiences in life. Everybody has the power to change how they respond to their life situations. Learning more constructive and compassionate ways to deal with life begins with mastering our relationship with the flow of thoughts in our heads. When we can control our preoccupations better, we respond to people and situations differently, and this ultimately helps us to feel better and more in control of our lives. Gaining increased mastery over our thoughts will bring a range of benefits such as feeling peaceful and happier on a more regular basis, boosting self-confidence and self-esteem, and enjoying better relationships. Reducing the chatter inside our heads is also known to improve sleep, mental and physical health and a wide array of other positive effects.

Self-care.

Looking after ourselves is essential when it comes to changing habits in our lives because when our lives are out of balance, this causes us anxiety which can make us more likely to go back to any old ways in dealing our problems. When we feel stressed cravings will likely get worse and any resolve to not use alcohol as a way of coping can lessen. Self-care will be discussed further in the following chapters but if you feel at a heightened risk of drinking it is always useful to check in with yourself before doing anything further. There are a range of negative emotions which may be underlying cravings for alcohol if you are not aware of the emotion you are experiencing. The acronym 'HALT BAD' can be used to give yourself a mental audit. If you identify with a feeling on the list, you can then work on meeting that need rather than going straight to alcohol.

HALT! Are you feeling **BAD**?

Are you feeling - **H**ungry? **A**ngry? **L**onely? **T**ired?

Or are you currently - **B**ored? **A**nxious? **D**epressed?

Recognising any of these feelings when you may be experiencing an urge to use alcohol can significantly reduce the power of the craving when you deal with the identified emotion.

Lifestyle changes.

When a person reduces or stops their alcohol use, it is likely that they will find themselves with more free time than they had before so considering how they will spend this time without alcohol can be incredibly helpful. Many people find taking up a new hobby or interest (or getting back into an old one) can be useful, others may use their time for volunteering, getting into a new exercise routine, working on business ideas or another project. Spending time by watching television, playing on your phone/ computer or being overly dependent on friends and family for your entertainment are high-risk strategies that may not be as lasting or beneficial to your emotional wellbeing. Do not underestimate the risk of experiencing boredom in your life as this will give you too much time to think about your old relationship with alcohol. When time passes and we forget about the worst aspects of our drinking habits, our brains can often romanticise about alcohol when we have too much free time available.

Learning a new skill, hobby or other creative use of your time will not only build your confidence and self-esteem but will allow you to establish a new identity with something that does not involve alcohol. Developing new interests and hobbies can also lead to building new friendships and opportunities for social interactions. Making new friends can be refreshing as you are now in control of how the other person views you, which does not need to comprise any judgements or pressure around alcohol use.

Relationships with people who know or share your old relationship with alcohol may be supportive in your goals with alcohol, or they may attempt to stop you from making long term changes. As discussed in Chapter 2, when one person in a relationship changes this can cause fear in the other person/ people about how the change will impact on your relationship with them, especially if they are not planning on making the same changes as you. Sometimes people in your life may not want you to change because it highlights and puts pressure on them to think about changing their own alcohol use.

Sometimes making changes to a person's lifestyle is not appealing because they enjoy the things that they do currently, or they would like to make changes but do not want to adjust their social schedule and associates. The nature of the person's motivation, level of confidence in their ability to change and the severity of alcohol use in their life will often predict whether they can make changes without changing their lifestyle. When people have tried this many times, they may need to revisit some lifestyle changes that can support their alcohol-related goals.

Support.

Everyone needs support in their lives, and this can be especially true when trying to maintain changes in your relationship with alcohol. The people most likely to succeed with long term changes will often be the people who have strong support from the people around them. Having adequate support does not require lots of people as the quality of your relationships is much more important than the quantity. Having a couple of good friends or supportive family members that you can trust can make a big difference when it comes to maintaining changes in your alcohol use. What exactly constitutes as good support may be an individual preference, but primarily the people around you should make you feel good when you are with them. Maybe they know you well and can remind you of your strengths, or they can listen without judging and telling you "what you should do".

Think about the people in your life and the strengths and qualities they can bring to your situation. Try and spend more time with the people who make you feel good and consider ways in which you may add positive support in your life if you think this is necessary.

Likewise, think about the people around you who cause you stress or make you feel unhappy, the people who drain your energy, talk to you or treat you badly or who are always negative about your life. It is crucial to plan how you will manage your encounters with these people so you can reduce any temptation to use alcohol as a coping response to negative emotions. Can you see this person less, or can you change the way you relate to them to reduce your distress when seeing them? The final chapters of this book may be able to help you learn new ways of reducing such stress.

If you feel you need to develop more supportive relationships in your life, you may find a local or online alcohol support group helpful or you may wish to develop other interests as discussed already. Women should be aware that many alcohol support groups can be male-dominated environments which can prove to be intimidating for women. While relationships among group members are strongly discouraged from developing it is inevitable that some women may feel uncomfortable in very male-dominated groups. Online communities may be safer in providing distance between members, but women should still be cautious about sharing too much information about themselves with anybody they meet online.

Healthy relationships.

When a person changes their involvement with alcohol, they may find that they need to reassess many of the relationships in their lives especially when alcohol has eroded a person's self-esteem or sense of self-confidence over many years. Healthy relationships are characterised by having mutual respect, trust and honesty, being able to work out problems together and feature compromise on both sides to understand each person's opinion or point of view. High levels of stress occur when relationships are out of balance with one person being more in control, and the other always giving way. Alcohol use can become a coping response to deal with troubled relationships in life, so if these are not adjusted and rebalanced, the person will be much more vulnerable to relapse.

Controlled/ Mindful drinking.

Mindful drinking is the practice of someone who may have previously used alcohol in a hazardous way but who can now control their use of alcohol in a way that reduces their overall harm. Research shows that some people who have problems with their alcohol use can implement strategies that lead to a more manageable pattern of drinking, but this typically requires a period of abstinence from alcohol for a month to help 'reset' the person's relationship with using alcohol.

For some people, this strategy can work long term; however, other people may find that they are unable to manage their drinking this way and decide it is better to aim for stopping using alcohol altogether. However you wish to proceed in your relationship with alcohol, it is useful to understand different situations which may arise where you may feel less control than at other times. Reviewing identified triggers, as covered in the previous chapter, can be useful when aiming to use alcohol with more thought and awareness.

FIONA STEELE

CHAPTER EIGHT: FAMILY MATTERS

Having problems with alcohol not only affects the person who is drinking but can impact every member of their family, even if they are not living together in the same household. Alcohol problems place family dynamics under a great deal of stress. Serious challenges families must deal with include events such as accidents, falls or other health problems, a member being charged with drink driving, experiencing violence or a range of other significant circumstances. Even when consequences are not as severe, the cumulative effect of living with a person who has problems with alcohol can be even more stressful and taxing on family members over time. Children and young people can especially find a parent's drinking stressful due to their age, level of understanding, and coping ability. This chapter will provide an overview of such issues and some ways in which to reduce stress levels for all family members.

Alcohol problems and family functioning.

A person who has issues with alcohol may not be able to give their full attention to other family members all of the time. A lack of connection with others can arise when a person is thinking about drinking alcohol, when they have consumed alcohol or when they are recovering physically and emotionally from their previous heavy use of alcohol. Others may experience drunken behaviour within their family as annoying, worrying, embarrassing, disruptive or unpredictable. Families can become isolated from their extended family or friends for the same reasons. Promises may be broken, finances for luxury activities may be depleted and special occasions such as birthday celebrations can become dreaded.

Routines such as bedtimes, mealtimes, and enjoying family time together may all be affected. Sometimes family rituals are continued physically, but they become like 'going through the motions' as the person drinking becomes less able to connect emotionally with the people around them. One of the criteria discussed in Chapter 4 examining alcohol dependence is recognising when alcohol becomes more of a priority for the person than other interests in their lives. Often this can gradually increase over time, leaving the person who is drinking to become more isolated from their family members, friends and the interests they once had.

Children from a young age may know that their parent is behaving strangely but will not understand the reasons why. Infants may express fear around a parent's unusual or erratic behaviours which increases their stress hormones and can impact on their long term physical and emotional development. Parental alcohol use can develop into a vicious cycle when a child's behaviour deteriorates due to experiencing stress, and a parent's alcohol use worsens as their way of coping with the increased pressure. Just as adults respond in different ways to a loved one's drinking problems, children and young people may also learn to cope in different ways with some strategies being considered healthier than others.

When children know there is something wrong with their family but do not have the brain capacity to understand alcohol problems, they can often feel like they are somehow to blame for their parent's drinking. Children may internalise this blame and develop issues around their confidence and self-esteem as they get older. Some children may believe that they can control their parent's drinking in some way by behaving in a specific manner, challenging them on their drinking behaviour, pouring away or hiding drink in the house. Adopting such strategies can generate a great deal of stress and misplaced feelings of responsibility in the process. Sometimes children may learn how to look after themselves and others from a young age and may develop a caring role for their parent or younger brothers and sisters. While this may result in these children learning how to care for others as adults, often it is at the expense of them valuing self-care and compassion. Some children may throw themselves into their schoolwork or activities that they can do outside of the home to limit any negative experiences with a parent drinking but may feel little attachment to their family as they mature. Sensitive young people can withdraw to their bedrooms, shutting down contact with their family and the outside world, so they do not have to deal with their family's problems. While this may be an effective short-term strategy for self-protection at home, the young person will likely be at an increased risk of developing problems in adult life. Such challenges can include self-harm behaviours, acquiring issues with alcohol or drugs or being more vulnerable to exploitation by others generally as they get older.

What helps children living in families with alcohol problems.

Often the frequency of drinking and the amount of alcohol consumed will be linked to how much pressure a family is experiencing and so if alcohol intake reduces then this is likely to reduce the resulting stress levels. If there are certain times when alcohol use is more likely to become problematic, children may be protected from the impact of their parent's drinking if they stay somewhere safer until their parents have recovered. Often parents believe they protect their children through hiding alcohol use, for example, by not drinking until their children have gone to bed. Having worked with many children and young people who have suffered as a result of their parent's alcohol use, I know how bad this strategy can be over time. Children usually know what their parents are doing long before it is openly discussed within a household. Many times, parents are unaware that their children have seen or heard things that are disturbing to them because the parent's secrecy around alcohol has taught the child that they cannot talk about this subject openly at home. Many children may feel too embarrassed, ashamed or worried to talk about their feelings to anyone as they often learn that having problems with alcohol is a taboo topic.

Stress levels for children living with a parent's alcohol problems can be relieved in several different ways.

-> Having another parent or trusted adult who can care for and physically respond to children when the parent who is drinking is unable.

-> Having honest conversations about alcohol allows children the opportunity to talk about how they are feeling as well as helping them to understand that their parent's drinking is not their fault or their responsibility.

-> Ensuring there are times when the family can enjoy activities together regularly when alcohol use can be limited.

-> Encouraging children to develop their strengths and interests can help increase their confidence and self-esteem as well as their opportunities for enjoyment and socialising with other children outside of the family home.

-> Help children to develop healthy coping responses to their problems in life by working with their problem-solving skills, attitude towards life and relaxation exercises for dealing with stress.

Many children would benefit from receiving support with a parent's drinking problems as these sorts of issues growing up can continue to affect people long after they have left their parental homes. Children can internalise stress when growing up with alcohol problems and form negative core beliefs about the world, which can be unhelpful to them as adults.

Children growing up in families experiencing chronic difficulties are at a much higher risk of experiencing a range of poor health and social outcomes in their adult life including unemployment, developing mental health, substance use or relationship problems. Research around adverse childhood experiences or ACEs, discussed in Chapter 2, continues to highlight the negative impact which parental issues can have on a child's development right into adulthood. For more information around this topic, search for Adverse Childhood Experiences online or follow the links from my website.

What helps adults living in families with alcohol problems.

If you are reading this as someone affected by a parent's drinking, no matter how long ago this was, it may be useful for you to seek further support if you feel you continue to be impacted by this as an adult. If you are living with another person's drinking problems currently, whether it be your partner, child or parent, it is crucial to make an effort to limit the stress levels you experience daily.

Experiencing high levels of stress over long periods can lead to a wide range of health problems, including increasing your chances of having a premature death. You can reduce your stress levels by adjusting your coping response and attitude towards a given situation or by making sure that you prioritise your own emotional wellbeing before attending to anybody else in your life.

You can't control another person having problems with alcohol, but you can control how you respond- what you do and how you think about it.

Confiding in a non-judgemental friend or being able to talk with others living in similar situations can be helpful. Support organisations aimed at helping family members affected by another person's drinking, such as Al-Anon, may have a local group in your area. Make time for activities which you enjoy and try to stick to healthy boundaries around respectful behaviour and communication within your family. Make sure you look after yourself through healthy eating, getting enough sleep, exercise and opportunities for relaxation. Try and let go of any feelings of responsibility to control, manage or look after somebody else who has problems with alcohol as far as possible.

How to talk about alcohol problems to others.

When speaking with children about alcohol problems, it is essential to be as honest as possible while remembering their age and capacity for understanding. Reassure children that it is not their problem and that they are not to blame. Help children understand that alcohol is something grown-ups drink for different reasons but that sometimes adults drink too much, and it makes them behave differently. Linking alcohol use with concerns your child might have about strange behaviours can be useful to help them understand that any concerning behaviour in their parent is not their fault.

An example conversation starter with a younger child might go as follows-

"When mummy feels ill/ when daddy shouts/ when mummy and daddy argue... it is because s/he has drunk too much alcohol and it's made them behave strangely. This is something that happens with adults at times and not for you to worry about. Mummy/ Daddy isn't very well at the minute but loves you very much and wants you to have a good life anyway/ not to worry about this/ talk to us about anything on your mind".

It can often help younger children to discuss their feelings through play, for example, by explaining how a teddy bear or doll might be feeling in certain situations rather than asking a child to express their thoughts directly. Teaching children the names of emotions and how they might experience these within their body (e.g. when I'm angry my body becomes tense and my heart races) can help children to identify and express their emotions more easily. Assisting children in learning how to identify feelings within themselves and other people increases their emotional intelligence and can be helpful when forming ways of managing the different emotions we can have in life.

Older children may be able to understand more information about alcohol, addiction and the reasons why you are drinking. Try not to burden children with too much information about adult difficulties that can cause them undue stress but being as truthful as possible can help them to piece together what they already know about a parent's alcohol use.

Often children and young people will not raise the topic of a parent drinking but might be relieved for somebody else to begin this conversation for them as they have many questions. Reassuring children and young people that other families are living with similar issues to theirs can help them to feel that they are not alone. Frequently children feel like their problems or their family is unique to them, so understanding that other young people might be living in families like theirs and are managing to have a good life anyway can be useful.

When talking to an adult about any problematic use of alcohol, it is essential not to blame, judge or criticise people on their drinking behaviour, as previously outlined in Chapter 5. When people feel criticised about their habits, they are much more likely to react with defence. This is why the more pressure we put on people to change the way they think or behave, the more we can increase their obstinance as a result. Discuss with someone about how they feel about their drinking and genuinely listen to what the person has to say. Try to remain non-judgemental and discover what meaning alcohol has for them. Talking about such topics with a spirit of curiosity and keeping an open mind may help you to learn new strengths and traits about the person you may have previously ignored. Chapter 5 examining how change happens should remind you of how difficult it can be for everybody to change bad habits and how meaningful changes rarely occur through preaching or ultimatums. Re-reading this chapter can help you with ideas on how to approach conversations around alcohol. Remember to check my website also for more information on all the topics covered so far.

FIONA STEELE

CHAPTER NINE: ALCOHOL AND MENTAL HEALTH

There often exists a close relationship between our drinking patterns and our mental health and emotional wellbeing. Alcohol use may worsen as a result of poor mental health, and in turn, heavy alcohol use can cause mental health problems. Whichever came first, when someone experiences difficulties with their alcohol use, mental health or both it is essential to look after each so that it does not impact the other.

Depression and anxiety.

Heavy alcohol use over time often results in increased symptoms of depression and anxiety for several different physiological and psychological reasons. Sometimes women may overlook or not recognise their symptoms of depression due to disguising it with alcohol use or through the necessity or determination to 'carry on regardless'. Depressive symptoms include experiencing overwhelming feelings of sadness, hopelessness, emptiness or worthlessness, which endure over time. Depression can impact a person's sleep by needing too much or getting too little, depletes their levels of energy and motivation, affects the ability to concentrate and can rob any enjoyment from a person's life.

Anxiety is characterised by overwhelming feelings of fear and nervousness about actual or imagined events occurring in our lives. At times people can feel anxious without understanding the reasons why but will experience a prevailing sense of something dreadful about to happen. The body experiences an increased heart rate, a dry mouth and inability to talk, difficulty concentrating, and thoughts might become rapid or jumbled. In severe instances, called panic attacks, a person may struggle for breath or feel as though experiencing a heart attack. Anxiety can impact on a person's sleep by not getting over to sleep or waking up too early through worrying. People with anxiety may find they avoid certain situations due to the possible risk of raising their anxiety levels, reducing the person's interests and activities significantly over time.

Alcohol use may be responsible for symptoms of depression and anxiety, and such symptoms often reduce over time following a reduction in alcohol use. For people who may be more dependent on alcohol use, stopping drinking may increase symptoms of depression and anxiety that can continue for weeks. It is always worth discussing your symptoms with a professional when they continue or worsen following a reduction in alcohol use. As discussed previously, stopping alcohol suddenly may cause severe withdrawal symptoms (that can prove fatal for some people). Should symptoms persist despite making improvements to your life and with your relationship to alcohol, then this may indicate a more severe issue that requires further assessment.

Negative thinking patterns.

Negative thinking and feelings often accompany excessive consumption of alcohol, and unhelpful thinking patterns can develop over time, making people feel stuck and unable to do anything about their situation. Consider how often you experience any of the negative thinking patterns outlined below. Understanding and identifying how we hold ourselves back is the first step to making any improvements to our lives.

Only seeing the negative.

People who routinely focus and dwell upon the unfavourable events and conditions of their lives will find over time that they become increasingly depressed and unsatisfied with life. By repeating any pattern over and over again, we train our brains to become better at this job and so it will find more and more negative things for you to become upset about, only making us feel worse.

It takes effort and practice to change any thinking style. Try to notice the favourable events and conditions of your life whenever possible. Regular practices such as creating a gratitude list every day can help you to think more optimistically with time. Attempting to stop yourself every time you think negatively and putting more effort into finding something encouraging about your situation can programme your brain to notice more positive aspects and help you to feel better generally.

Jumping to conclusions.

Jumping to conclusions can include a great variety of things such as:

-> worrying about things that haven't happened

-> thinking that we know what somebody else is

thinking or

doing (and it's always something bad)

-> taking everything that happens personally

-> believing we can predict the future

-> assuming the worst will happen.

Often when people are feeling low and emotionally vulnerable, they may ruminate about the worst that can happen, take everything to heart and form many assumptions which make them feel even worse by increasing the stress reaction in the body. This physiological response confirms to the brain that there is something wrong and so the mind and body work together to help perpetuate negative thinking.

As discussed, having awareness of when we are thinking in unhelpful ways is the first step in being able to change our mindset. Applying effort to change the way we think on a regular basis will change our brain pathways to become more in tune with our desired outlook over time.

Black and white thinking.

Black and white thinking refers to only being able to see the world in terms of distinct polarities such as black or white/ good or bad/ all or nothing. Thinking like this prevents us from understanding and accepting the many possibilities that lie between these extremes.

This way of thinking is common in people experiencing depression and frequently reflected when people relapse into old behaviours after a small set back. Black and white thinking can lead us to never feeling like we are good enough/ have enough/ do enough/ be enough. If we do not consider everything to be perfect with ourselves, with other people or with the conditions of our life, then we can feel like we have failed and that there is no point in continuing with our efforts. Thinking like this often results in a person developing low self-esteem and confidence as they never match up to the ideals they have set.

If you feel you may suffer from black and white thinking at times, try to recognise when you are doing this and make an effort to retrain yourself by thinking of alternatives which exist in the centre-ground.

Some examples might include:

Black & white thinking	Alternative way of thinking
'I can never change my drinking habits'.	'I haven't changed yet, but with the right skills and support, it has been possible for other people, and therefore it is possible for me'.
'I'll never cope without alcohol in my life'.	'There was a time in my life when I coped ok without alcohol, and I can learn to do that again' **or** 'There are some new ways of coping listed in this book I haven't tried yet which might work for me'.

'All my friends will fall out with me if I stop drinking alcohol'.	'Some of my friends may not see me as much when I stop drinking, but I will make an effort to find other ways to keep in touch with them' **or** 'Perhaps it is time in my life to find friends who want to spend time together without alcohol'.

How to manage unhelpful thinking.

Recognising when we our thoughts are destructive and choosing to think differently is the key to changing how we feel. Try to rationalise what you are thinking and query whether it is based more on fact or imagination.

If you can, put your thoughts through the following tests:

-> Is there any evidence for seeing things this way?

-> Is there any other way of looking at this situation?

-> What would I say to a friend if they were thinking this way about a similar situation?

Perhaps there is evidence and merit in thinking the way you are thinking but is there anything you can do to change what is happening? When the answer is no, then this is something you need to learn how to relinquish, together with the stories created by our imagination.

In situations like these, or when rationalising with your thoughts won't work, there are ways in which you can learn to separate yourself from and let go of your speculations. Ways of relaxing and relieving tension such as using breathing exercises or practising meditation, listening to soothing music or speaking with someone you trust, walking outdoors and performing yoga are all proven to be beneficial in helping people manage unhelpful thoughts.

Grounding yourself in the present moment can also be helpful when your thoughts are racing, and you are feeling overwhelmed. Touch something close to you and notice how it feels- is it cold or warm, soft or hard- appreciate the texture of the surface for a minute. Feel the ground below your feet or the seat supporting where you are sitting currently. Scan parts of your body and focus on releasing any tension you may be experiencing while slowing down your breathing. If you feel as though you need to release pent up agitation, you may find jumping, shaking your limbs or beating your chest helpful as ways of rebalancing.

Think about some things you might find helpful or consider if any of the ways listed above might appeal to you in learning new ways of managing your thoughts.

Self-esteem

Heavy use of alcohol is often entwined with a person's feelings of low self-esteem. While self-esteem issues may have influenced alcohol becoming problematic for a person, many times, heavy alcohol use will erode a person's sense of self-worth over time. There are many reasons for this, but heavy alcohol use can often come along with considerable regrets, strained relationships and trying to reconcile alcohol-related choices and behaviours with the person whom we believe ourselves to be.

Low self-esteem manifests in many ways but generally involves feelings of low self-worth and believing the value and needs of others as more important than our own. Some people find they are always giving way to the people around them; they may be particularly sensitive to other people's opinions of them and can be more accepting of abusive or unhealthy relationships. Women with low self-esteem are more likely to be victims of violence than women possessing higher self-worth, and this can increase significantly when consuming alcohol.

Low self-esteem can impact every area of your life and will reduce the amount of enjoyment, happiness and motivation experienced in daily activities. Feelings of low self-esteem can influence a person to drink more excessively and they may come to rely more heavily on alcohol use over time. Low self-confidence can also significantly reduce a person's capability to control or stop drinking alcohol.

Self-esteem may be enhanced though following the advice and guidance contained within this book regarding the importance of self-care, learning new ways to deal with stress and becoming more competent in managing our thoughts, which in turn helps us to feel better and more in control of our lives. There are many other ways of improving self-esteem, so I have included more links on my website, and will discuss this topic further in the next chapter.

Social media and mental health

Women are currently experiencing worse mental health and self-esteem than has ever been recorded previously. This is especially true of younger women and research has shown a clear correlation between symptoms of depression and the number of hours spent using social media daily. Quite frankly, it does not take a researcher to tell anyone who has immersed themselves on these platforms how bad social media can be for our self-esteem. Indeed, platform is an appropriate word, as social media is often used to 'stage' how people would like others to imagine their lives.

Young women may be particularly impressionable as they are still learning about the world and forming their personalities. Rather than looking to the people who are naturally surrounding them and forming a holistic sense of character based on values, self-worth and family or community connections; social media presents a global platform offering a one-dimensional understanding of identity based on how a person visually represents. Young women often feel they must convey a certain image or indulge in popular crazes to be accepted and may be subjected to intense bullying when seen as not conforming. Unfortunately, this can result in some people placing more importance to how they look and being liked on social media rather than developing personality traits of kindness and empathy or taking the time to make genuine friendships in real life.

Limit the time you spend on social media, understand that it is all mostly fake anyway and go about making yourself a life that makes you feel good, regardless of how others are spending their time 'staging' their lives.

Five ways to wellbeing.

Research carried out in the UK has concluded that there are five key ways in which we can improve our mental health and emotional wellbeing. People who regularly practise these things report greater satisfaction with their lives, higher levels of self-esteem and better physical health. Each of the five areas is important to a well-balanced life. Consider which of these areas you could enhance to improve your contentment with the world. I have suggested some ways in which you can think about the different areas to help you determine what actions you would like to take.

Be active

Find an exercise you would enjoy doing more in life. Even dancing to your favourite music for five minutes can lift your mood and could help with weight loss when done regularly over time. Take your children out to a new playpark or play some sports with them. Go dog walking with a friend or set reminders on your phone to get up and move about every hour.

Connect

Connect with others, yourself and the world around you. Spend less time worrying and focus your energy on improving your relationships. Make time for self-care activities, practice self-love and compassion and get out into nature. Get more involved with your community, attend local events and get to know other people in your area.

Take notice

Pay attention to what is going on around you. When

people speak to you, make a habit of trying not to think about other things and give them your undivided attention. Take a look at the sky and notice the sunset, the birds singing or the colours of nature. Check-in with yourself throughout the day and focus on releasing any tension or worries you are experiencing.

Keep learning

Make time to learn about the things which interest you. You can complete research online, find out if there is a class nearby or ask other people who know more than you. Find out about other people's interests in life and what makes them excited. Ask your family members or friends to introduce you to their favourite hobbies or skills and try them out together.

Give

Think about ways in which you can help other people or give back to your family or community. Maybe you have a particular skill you can share, or you're especially good at something, and other people would find this helpful. Think about ways in which you can contribute towards improving the environment or your local area. Spend time caring for a pet or tending plants.

CHAPTER TEN: ALCOHOL AND SPIRITUALITY

What is spirituality?

When people talk about spirituality, all sorts of images and ideas may come to mind. Some people might immediately think that spirituality means the same as religion, while others may think it is something too 'far out' or just not their sort of thing. In truth, spirituality relates to having a belief that we are part of something bigger than ourselves. Such convictions may develop from religious teachings or a personal interpretation of an ultimate force in life whether you call this God, Tao, Mother Nature, Source, Universal Energy or your Guardian Angels.

Spirituality involves asking ourselves more profound questions about our existence such as 'Who am I?' and 'What is the point of me being here?' and then forming an answer to these questions that brings us a sense of peace and unity with the world we live within.

When we only focus on the material aspects of the world, our happiness and self-esteem rely on external factors like owning beautiful things, looking a certain way or boasting about our lives to others on social media. We are continually comparing and scoring ourselves against the people around us, meaning our feelings of self-worth and value are reliant on how well we think we are doing in this 'race' with others. We might feel as though we need more out of life before we will feel happy. As mentioned in Chapter 1, this is how advertising works to sell us 'things' which they promise will make us 'happier' in some way.

Why does spirituality matter?

Just as 'tomorrow never comes', happiness does not come with the things that we are yet to have. Instead, this develops from how we feel about ourselves in the world we live in, in this current moment. Where religion and spirituality may differ is that religion often teaches us that we must do a particular thing or live a certain way in this life with an emphasis on achieving peace and salvation when we transition into our afterlife. Spirituality emphasises attaining inner peace in this lifetime, and we may find this in many ways, including through religious teachings. Spirituality does not require us to go anywhere or to do anything special but guides us towards recognising our inner or true nature, who we are at our essence.

When people develop a sense of spirituality, with whichever belief they most resonate, they may feel more intrinsically supported, guided and nurtured than before. Many people report increased feelings of strength in life from having a sense that a 'Higher Power' is assisting us in dealing with our problems or that there is a 'bigger picture' which we do not currently understand.

When people become spiritually aligned, there comes an understanding that **we are all perfectly fine as we are**, and this can bring feelings of peace and contentment despite individual life circumstances. Through cultivating peace within ourselves and with the events of our lives, people who have few material possessions can feel more ease and contentment than people with vast material wealth.

While spirituality encourages us to look within ourselves for the answers we need in life; it also allows us to feel a deeper connection with others and the world in which we live. We realise that we are all intrinsically connected as being a part of this bigger picture and develop more compassion and appreciation for ourselves, the people around us and the world in which we live as a result.

Meaning and purpose.

Many people can struggle with finding a sense of meaning and purpose in life. Our families and society might wish to direct our ambitions towards being married or having children; owning property or having a successful career but what happens when we don't have these things or when we do have them but still find ourselves unfulfilled? Just as happiness does not come from the things which we have, our purpose in life cannot be dictated to us by others. Having a sense of purpose in life is strongly associated with our feelings of happiness. Spirituality would guide us to finding such meaningful answers by searching within ourselves.

Very often our unhappiness in life comes from the thoughts we are thinking and the things which we tell ourselves. If we have a negative view of ourselves or we engage in unhelpful thinking patterns, this can cause us unnecessary emotional pain that can affect every part of our lives. As we discussed in the previous chapter, experiencing such blocks can both increase our reliance on alcohol and work against us in our efforts in cutting down or stopping using alcohol. If you recognise this to be an aspect of your life, it can be helpful to work through these thought processes with a professional or check out the extra resources for Chapter 9 on my website.

Everybody needs to feel valued and that their life has significance whether this is developed through a spiritual understanding or in some other way. Caring for family or engaging in service to others; creating art, music or leaving some other legacy for the world or looking after the earth and her wildlife are just some of the ways people may find meaning in their lives. Our emotions can help guide us to finding meaning if we learn to recognise what thoughts and activities make us feel alive and happy.

Questions you might ask yourself to get closer to your own purpose and contribution are:- What is it you are good at or enjoy doing? What excites or fascinates you in life? When are the moments that you become so absorbed in what you are doing that you don't notice the time passing? What do other people ask you to do or feel you are talented in doing?

Of course, we may not always be able to do what it is we would love to do in life due to our circumstances. Cultivating any opportunities available through which to align with what makes us feel happy, will help us to feel more satisfied and content with our lives overall.

Alcohol and spirituality.

As we have discussed throughout this book, alcohol can be experienced in a similar way to an anaesthetic. Alcohol can be used to deaden the pain of existence and can also stop us from taking the actions necessary to improve our circumstances. Inaction may come through procrastination and putting the required changes off until tomorrow or through denial and not accepting things as having the impact that they are. Alcohol numbs our pain, but often we need to feel discomfort for us to make changes in our lives. Just as physical pain can be a signal that something in our body requires attention and emotional pain can signal a need to focus on correcting unhelpful thinking patterns, existential suffering is a signal that our soul is calling out for attention.

Existential pain relates to the suffering people can experience, which is not directly related to their physical or mental health but comes from a lack of meaning and purpose as we have discussed. While alcohol can often distract us from thinking about or finding such meaning for ourselves, it can also add to our distress over time as we may feel a further disconnection from ourselves and others through embarrassing and uncharacteristic alcohol-related behaviours and situations.

Alcoholics Anonymous

There are many alcohol support programmes which include elements of spirituality, the most well-known being Alcoholics Anonymous or AA. Alcoholics Anonymous follows a 12-step programme and strongly encourages members to develop a relationship with God to help them move forward in a life without alcohol. Some people find the religious aspects to AA very helpful, and AA has helped many people to stop drinking and develop more meaning to their lives. For other people, however, the religious aspect of AA does not resonate with them, and they may not find the same benefits in attending meetings. Alcoholics Anonymous, as we have mentioned in Chapter 7, may be perceived as being a male-dominated organisation. Not only will this be apparent at most meetings but with the religious element of the programme being based on Christian teachings, these often do not resonate with women in the same way as men.

Religion and women.

Christian teachings, like other dominant world religions, place women as being secondary to men and expect women to be submissive to men and their religious doctrine. Many revered texts are generally not kind towards women, and such scriptures are responsible for many atrocities committed towards women both historically and in the present day. Dominant religions all have men at the tops of their institutions- from their interpretations of God or Allah, their prophets, their heads of churches right down to clergy on a local level. While many women may develop their own spiritual beliefs within dominant religions, for others, these deep-rooted ideas of women's subservience to men may be troublesome.

In other traditions such as within many indigenous cultures and Pre-Christian religions, called paganism, women are exalted, and 'Mother'  Earth takes the top spot as being the Ultimate Creator. Women are often regarded as sacred and divine Goddesses deeply connected with Nature. Women's roles within their families and communities are as equally respected as men's and many women possessed unique talents of healing and fore-telling abilities.

Societies supporting strong religious dogmas tell us that paganism is evil, and that 'witches' were burnt alive for working with the devil. Men have suppressed women's innate talents and abilities for centuries. Nevertheless, women have not lost this ability to connect with our Source, channel the divine and heal ourselves, our families and communities.

How to connect with your spiritual essence.

Every person on this earth can tune into their spiritual essence if this is something they wish to develop, and they are willing to spend time and energy learning. As mentioned at the start of this chapter, all the answers to your questions lie within you. When we quieten our minds from its endless chatter and take our focus away from the external factors of our lives, we are then able to tune into a quiet part of ourselves which contains all the answers to our questions. Answers may come to you as if they are being whispered from a wiser version of yourself or they may appear as images or as a deep sense of knowing. Tuning into this inner wisdom may be thought of as developing your intuition, and your ability to see the bigger picture in your life will increase.

Often, we only recognise our intuition about a person or situation as being correct after an event has happened. We talk about not having the benefit of 'hindsight', but if we were to tune into our inner wisdom regularly, we could develop a better sense of 'foresight' within our lives. Learning how to connect with our inner wisdom is one of the primary aims of learning and practising meditation and meditation is one of the best-known routes for people to develop their spiritual nature. There are many different types of meditation, and these will be explored further in the Chapter 10 resource section on my website.

While meditation is one of the best-known routes, it is certainly not the only route available to us when we wish to tap into our innate knowledge and wisdom. People can find that answers will come to them while they are engaging in other pursuits, especially those they find absorbing and do not think about the external stresses of their lives. It may be through an activity such as dancing, running, creating art or music, cooking, taking a bath, watching the sunset or playing with our children. Ideas that would improve our lives can also come to us in moments throughout the day, but often we ignore these or shut them down before realising the wisdom and truth they may hold for us.

Developing a sense of spirituality can provide you with a framework from which you can more fully experience life, strengthen your sense of identity, self-esteem and self-compassion as well as finding more connection with the people around you. You could say it is an excellent antidote to alcohol problems.

All the answers you seek are within you- it is only a matter of learning how to listen and trust yourself.

FIONA STEELE

ABOUT THE AUTHOR

Fiona has written this book after learning about alcohol and other drugs through her personal, professional and academic experiences gathered over 20 years.

Fiona has supported countless people to gain better control of their substance use and has trained numerous addiction professionals with her unique, down-to-earth style. Fiona currently lives in Belfast, N. Ireland.

For further information and to contact Fiona visit her website at:
www.fionasteele.com

Printed in Great Britain
by Amazon